Let's Read About Our Bodies

Mouth

by Cynthia Klingel* and Robert B. Noyed
photographs by Gregg Andersen

Amoroso is preferred name

Reading consultant: Cecilia Minden-Cupp, Ph.D.,
Adjunct Professor, College of Continuing and Professional Studies, University of Virginia

For a free color catalog describing Weekly Reader® Early Learning Library's list of high-quality books, call 1-800-542-2595 or fax your request to (414) 332-3567.

Library of Congress Cataloging-in-Publication Data

Klingel, Cynthia.
    Mouth / by Cynthia Klingel and Robert B. Noyed.
       p. cm. — (Let's read about our bodies)
    Includes bibliographical references and index.
    Summary: An introduction to the mouth, what it is used for, and how to take care of it.
    ISBN 0-8368-3067-9 (lib. bdg.)
    ISBN 0-8368-3156-X (softcover)
    1. Mouth—Juvenile literature. [1. Mouth.] I. Noyed, Robert B. II. Title.
  QM306.K553   2002
  611'.31—dc21   2001055053

This edition first published in 2002 by
Weekly Reader® Early Learning Library
330 West Olive Street, Suite 100
Milwaukee, WI 53212 USA

An Editorial Directions book
Editors: E. Russell Primm and Emily Dolbear
Art direction, design, and page production: The Design Lab
Photographer: Gregg Andersen
Weekly Reader® Early Learning Library art direction: Tammy Gruenewald
Weekly Reader® Early Learning Library production: Susan Ashley

Printed in the United States of America

1 2 3 4 5 6 7 8 9 06 05 04 03 02

Note to Educators and Parents

As a Reading Specialist I know that books for young children should engage their interest, impart useful information, and motivate them to want to learn more.

Let's Read About Our Bodies is a new series of books designed to help children understand the value of good health and taking care of their bodies.

A young child's active mind is engaged by the carefully chosen subjects. The imaginative text works to build young vocabularies. The short, repetitive sentences help children stay focused as they develop their own relationship with reading. The bright, colorful photographs of children enjoying good health habits complement the text with their simplicity and both entertain and encourage young children to want to learn — and read — more.

These books are designed to be used by adults as "read-to" books to share with children to encourage early literacy in the home, school, and library. They are also suitable for more advanced young readers to enjoy on their own.

— *Cecilia Minden-Cupp, Ph.D.,*
Adjunct Professor, College of Continuing and
Professional Studies, University of Virginia

This is my mouth.

I can eat with
my mouth.

I can talk with
my mouth.

I can kiss my doll with my mouth.

I can smile with
my mouth.

My teeth are in my mouth. I brush my teeth every morning and every night.

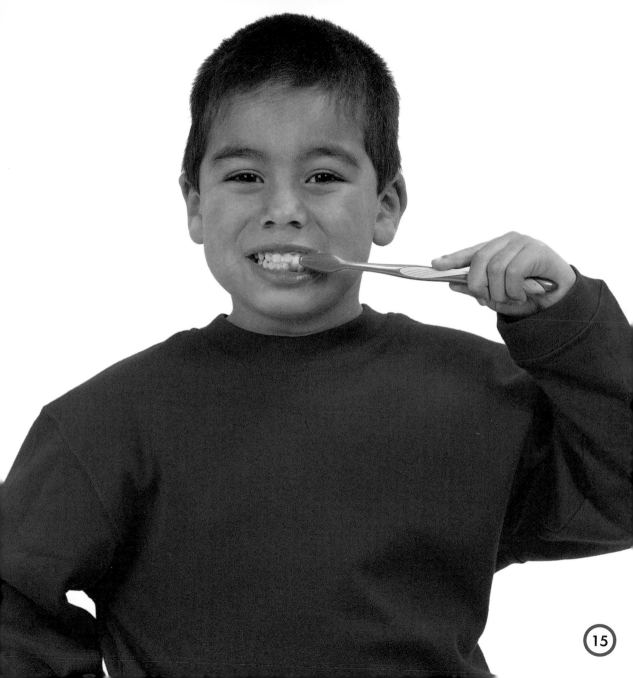

I take care of my mouth. I go to the dentist.

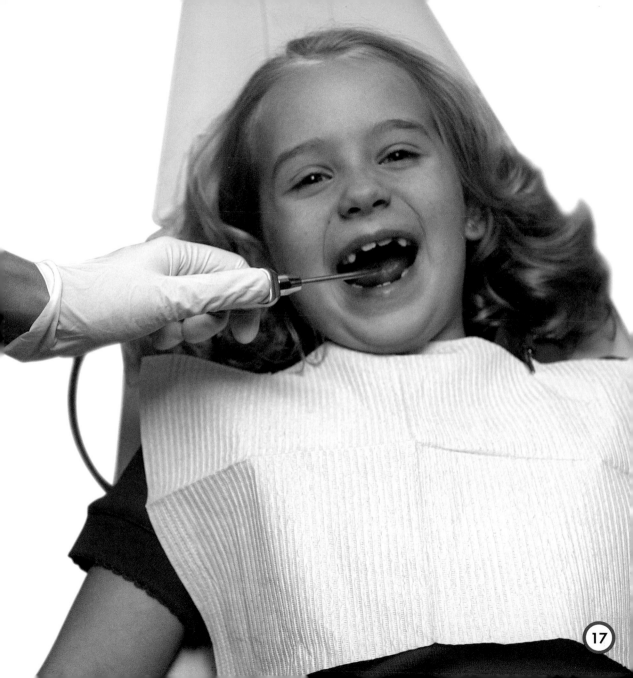

The dentist helps keep my teeth clean and healthy.

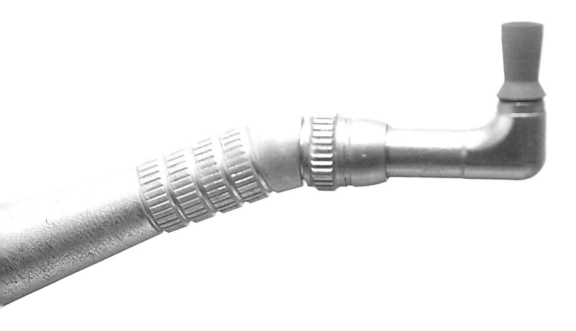

I can make funny faces with my mouth!

Glossary

dentist—a doctor who cares for the teeth and mouth

healthy—good for the body

teeth—the hard, bony parts of the mouth used to bite and chew

For More Information

Fiction Books

Faulkner, Keith. *The Wide-Mouthed Frog.* New York: Dial
   Books for Young Readers, 1996.

Grohman, Almute, and Patricia Bereck Weikersheimer. *Dragon
   Teeth and Parrot Beaks: Even Creatures Brush Their Teeth.*
   Carol Stream, Ill.: Quintessence Publishing Co., 1998.

Nonfiction Books

Moses, Brian. *Munching, Crunching, Sniffling, and Snooping.*
   New York: DK Publishing, 1999.

Web Sites
What Is Spit?
kidshealth.org/kid/talk/yucky/spit.html
To learn why we have saliva in our mouths

Index

About the Authors

Cynthia Klingel has worked as a high school English teacher and an elementary school teacher. She is currently the curriculum director for a Minnesota school district. Cynthia Klingel lives with her family in Mankato, Minnesota.

Robert B. Noyed started his career as a newspaper reporter. Since then, he has worked in school communications and public relations at the state and national level. Robert B. Noyed lives with his family in Brooklyn Center, Minnesota.